Witness
Appalachia to Hatteras
The Gilbert-Chappell Distinguished Poets
& Student Poets
2017

Edited by
Ted Wojtasik

Front cover art: William Parker
Design and typesetting: Ted Wojtasik
Proofreader: Abigail Yates

Acknowledgements

*We would like to thank the North Carolina Poetry Society,
the Gilbert-Chappell Distinguished Poets Series, the North
Carolina Center for the Book, Molly Westmoreland,
Michael Beadle, William Blackley, Laurie Gilbert Sandford,
Dick Gilbert, the editorial board of the St. Andrews
University Press, and St. Andrews University for their
support of the GCDP and this book project.*

ISBN-13: 978-0998194974
ISBN-10: 0998194972

SA
UNIVERSITY
PRESS

St. Andrews University Press

St. Andrews University
(A Branch of Webber International University)
1700 Dogwood Mile
Laurinburg, NC 28352
press@sa.edu
(910) 277-5310

Dedicated to

Michael Beadle

Whose vision will sustain the Gilbert-Chappell
Distinguished Poets Series for future years

Table of Contents

Western Region: Appalachia 1

Pat Riviere-Seel

Desire 3

From the Almanac of Broken Things 4

How to Get Where You Need to Go 5

Living with the Dead 6

The Bears 7

What Emmett Saw 8

Mary Coggins

How It Feels 11

Mom and Dad 12

My Foster Family 13

I Forgave Him 14

Tom 15

Jade Shuler

The Home That I Couldn't Call Home 17

Hammer and Nails 18

Roses 19

Break-Up Letter 20

Chemistry 21

Benjamin J. Cutler

Deathbed Fashion Show 23
Moon Clippings for Birds 25
On Teaching (Not Preaching) Poetry 26
Grendel's Mom 27
Dead Bird Poem 29

Cathy Larson Sky

Prey 31
Chickens 32
Fish Magic 34
Eye Light 35
Salt 37

Central Region: The Sandhills 39

Ruth Moose

Leaving the Lake House with the Blue Door 41
Circe, On-Line Shopper 42
Circe in a Cream Negligee with Matching Pom Pom
Sling Back Stiletto Slippers (Victoria's Secret $170) 44
Circe in Jeans 7 for Mankind ($290) 45
Circe in a Royal Blue Suit (Armani $3950) 46
Circe in Widow's Weeds (Neiman Marcus $2899) 47
In the Bell Tower (Oxford England) 48
The Wasps 50

Daily Tasks of My Cat, Patrick 51

Trees I Have Known 52

Molly Porter

How to Breathe 53

Passive 55

Apprehensive 56

Sophia Iannuzzi

Waffle House 57

There is No Softness in Florida 59

Best Served Warm 60

Thirst 61

Esmeralda Garcia

The Chime 63

Ready For 64

The Moment of Bliss 65

Disagreeing Views 66

Douglas Chapman

Dad's Last List 67

Milkweed Journey 69

On the Stillness of Trees 70

The Gift of Loss 71

Eastern Region: Hatteras 73

Amber Flora Thomas

Damaged Photos 75
The Age of Forgetting 76
The Old Horse 77
The Moon That Night 78
Pollen 79
A Wild Thing 80

Tevin Aitken

We Sit by the Bonfire 81
Life is a Journey 82
You're the Judge 83
The First Knock at the Door was Strange 84
Moment of Happiness 86

S.L. Cockerille

To the Bone 87
History's Glare 89

John Gray

Name 91
Twenty Three 92
DHS Class of '64 93

SERVING COUNTRY—DAY 1035—Tear Drops on a Little Green Bird 94

DS—THE END 96

A Note on the Gilbert-Chappell Distinguished Poets Series * 109

Western Region: Appalachia

Pat Riviere-Seel, Distinguished Poet

Mary Coggins, High School Student Poet

Jade Shuler, High School Student Poet

Benjamin J. Cutler, Adult Student Poet

Cathy Larson Sky, Adult Student Poet

Desire

"From this roof in this city, once upon a time, you could pretend to be anything you wanted to be."
　　　　　—DeNeen L. Brown, *Washington Post*, December 31, 2007

Pat Riviere-Seel

We were walking through Georgetown,
back to my car after dinner when
a man called to you, "Senator!
Flowers for your lady?" You shook
your head as we walked faster, laughing.

I wanted you to buy the flowers,
but you were no senator,
and I was not your lady.
We had spent hours wandering
side streets, reading menus
saying we didn't care what we ate.

True enough. We just needed something
to keep ourselves upright and separated—
swallowing steaming mussels dripping butter,
salty and sweet as afternoon kisses.

From the Almanac of Broken Things

I choose this earth that breaks
my heart again and again,

the woods for the way trees
bend, fall, and return to dirt.

I choose the sand dollar, the nautilus
that in brokenness find new creation.

I choose the favorite doll that no longer cries,
loved into silence and rags.

I choose the memory of a stranger's touch
that lifted my face above water. Because

I did not drown, I choose morning,
the gauzy-gray dawn that returns.

I choose the once-wild Palomino
whose beauty can never be tamed.

I choose light from long dead stars
that illuminates without heat.

I choose March with its promise of spring,
the warm days that tease, the blizzard

that insulates and warms the bulbs, the seeds,
all that lies beneath the surface, waiting.

How to Get Where You Need to Go

Start with gratitude. Start with the bug
that crawled across your napkin, the one
you thought was a centipede before you counted
legs. Or start with the first conscious breath you took
before you opened your eyes, before
you became aware of waking.
Bless the bug, bless the breath.
Keep practicing gratitude for the small things.
Unhitch the rusty trailer of expectations.
It's too heavy a load for a Kia Soul to pull.
Trade in your Kia for a white convertible,
toss out all the maps, disable the GPS, and just drive.
Take a wrong turn, a left turn, a right turn.
Turn onto a gravel road and sing. Turn up the volume,
turn in to your life, the one you've been waiting for.

Living with the Dead

My husband's upstairs working on his fifth
draft for a memoir class. He hadn't intended
to write about his late wife,
but there she emerged out of the free write.
I'm in my study going down that dark
rabbit hole with Jimmie, love of my 30s
when we thought ourselves all grown up.

The house is getting crowded these days,
filled with Maggi's constant chatter,
Jimmie's braying laugh, the two of them
carrying on in the living room, no doubt
cracking jokes at our expense. How foolish
we must seem to them now. Maybe they
pity us from their vantage point
in the afterlife. Ed and I are, after all,
sadly mortal, struggling with how
to honor the dead and get the details right.

All Maggi and Jimmie want to do is gossip.
We're not sure how long they intend to stay,
but hope they don't plan on taking up residence.
This arrangement could get awkward after awhile.
Still, truth be known, I rather enjoy having them
around.

At least they're not cleaning out
the fridge and drinking all the Scotch.

The Bears

The bears returned last night.
The mother and her three cubs
slept in the mound of leaves.

They left deep indentations
where summer-sated bellies
and substantial paws lay curled
beneath the maple's outstretched limbs
and the quarter moon's pale light.

All day, while I raked leaves into piles,
the bears were watching. They moved
silent and unseen among evergreens,
gray trunks, and branches as they had
all summer. Preparing for winter sleep,
they stuffed themselves on acorns and grubs.

One late summer day they came into
the orchard. The cubs shimmied
up the young apple trees, bent
one bough to the ground and broke
another in their play. The mother
took her time selecting fallen apples,
and those she could reach balanced
on her hind legs. She carried these
one by one to her cubs, gently
urged them to taste and chew.
Who knows how long winter will last?

What Emmett Saw

I outran a storm as he took aim,
his lens focused on distant clouds.
Next morning my anonymous back
appeared in black and white, front page,
local section. *Gathering Storm,* the caption read.

I held a backbend till my spine
almost snapped so he could photograph
my profile against the setting sun.
I mounted rooftops, shook
my rusty curls over staircase railings.
I shimmied into trees and once sat
hours under white lights, watching him
watch me. Behind the bellows
he framed a girl whose portrait
won him best in show. It hangs now

on my bedroom wall, passport
to the days with Emmett,
who embraced grassy slopes,
winter limbs, captured
the woman I was becoming.

It was the year I exploded—
my first husband, gone
before I turned twenty. Good
sense abandoned, I coiled,
a copperhead ready to sink my fangs
into kindness—showed up drunk
or stoned, canceled dates,

used every curse word I knew
but banished all endearments.
Emmett endured.

I did everything he asked,
even walked the railroad trestle
at dawn in a white bikini—
stumbling, heavy with sleep,
my feet perched on a metal rail
and nothing below but air.

How It Feels

Mary Coggins

Stillness and silence
sinking down deep
settling in my heart
without a peep
with fake friends acting their parts
lying and knowing they're doing wrong
memories and a happy time
reading it like a line
depression is all of this
so make a wish
have hope for love to fill your head
somehow giving you less time to dread
now open your eyes
and see all the lies.

Mom and Dad

The word "mom" means many things
It means love and hope
It means protection
Waking up in the middle of the night because her
baby had a nightmare
Holding her children through the tears
Holding them through their laughs.

The word "mom" only means one thing to me
Heartbreak ...
Because she never protected me
Or held me through my tears or laughter
My mom was just not there.

The word "dad" means many things
It means reading bedtime stories to your babies.
It means nights full of games and mornings full of
delight.

The word "dad" only means one thing to me
Heartbreak ...
Because he left me alone
He didn't even give me the chance to say goodbye
He gave me nightmares of him never coming back
He made the nightmares real
My dad just left me.

My Foster Family

Gratitude for a family that is not my own
taking me in for the nights to come
loving me even though I'm broken
Broken from a life of constant pain from my family before
From my own blood
My foster parents
they smile when I come home
their laughter rings high with mine when I feel alone
gratitude for a family that loves me more than my own
they have moved into my heart
gratitude for my family
That's what they have become
as misfit as they are
My foster parents and I
I am happy to see their faces
I am hopeful to hear their laughter
I am whole in my broken pieces
I am home

I Forgave Him

I forgave the man that hurt me in my childhood
that haunted my dreams.
I forgave the man that followed me through the
night
that took me from my home until first light.
I forgave the man that hurt me
physically and emotionally,
The man that made me strong
yes, that man did wrong.
However, I forgave that man.

Tom

He wasn't always an evil man.
He had good intentions
bright dreams for the future.
Before me
my mom
my family
he had one of his own. He planned to marry, then tragedy
struck.
The mother of a daughter that wasn't quite his, but he loved
them both,
gone in the night.

So down the road that was paved with good intentions he
went
until one night at a gas station
a woman with red hair caught his eye.
That was the beginning,
the start of a descent into madness
the beginning of our story,
leading him to be the evil man he was to me.

The Home That I Couldn't Call Home

Jade Shuler

Treading through the door,
you can tell a family lives here.
There are picture frames strewn in every direction.
Photos of smiling children,
all in various stages of toothlessness.
The air is happy and still.
It is warmed by the mid afternoon sun, it is filled with
chatter.
Outside, the trees are different.
The trees are not chatting amongst family,
they are dead.
Trees can die from loneliness, just as people can.
Last nights rain, has seeped through each of the tree's
years.
All the way to the heart.
The rain left the tree in frozen rigidness.
Inside, the crackling fire and engaging conversations
boil with laughter.
Sweetness is baking.
The warm aroma wafts through the kitchen, and escapes
into the room.

Hammer and Nails

It is in shambles, it is broken.
This family, this house
Is a decaying mess.
This house creaks with every move,
The foundation is rotten.
The house is no longer mine,
It is only a roof with four walls holding it up.

My sister, too young to remember
The amount of happiness before, dreams.
Only in REM
Does she experience happiness.
Our father abandoned us,
How do I explain to a child,
Divorce?

My own rage does not benefit her,
I cannot fix her broken innocence.
All that I can do is get to work.
With my hammer and nail, put this house back together,
One stable floorboard after another,
Making it a loving home yet again.
There will be hope for happiness,
As long as I have my hammer and nails.

Roses

Roses were in full bloom
The day of my birth.
They were as innocent and pure
As the first breath I took.
"Rose" is part of the name given to me.
Oh, how unfair it is.
That a person who is so flawed,
Was given a name with such purity to withhold.

Roses were in full bloom
The day my family started to fall apart.
They were as delicate
As the words he fed me as to why.
"Rose" is part of the name given to me.
I am not a rose, but Rose is a part of me.

Break-Up Letter

Dear chronic social anxiety:
I no longer wish to call you mine.

You make tasks I need to complete,
Dress themselves as feats I must overcome.
I am kicking you out, your suitcase will be out front.

Anxiety, you cripple me;
Your vengeance is clear and misguided,
Your attacks leave me dizzy and faint,
Unable to perform oral reports.

Anxiety, you cripple me;
You prevent me from making new friends
And make maintaining the friendships I have
exhausting.

I have tried to ebb your attack
Using meditational breathing:
Breathe in.
Hold.
Breathe out.
But you remain relentless.
Now, I am kicking you out.
Get your suitcase, I have a car out front.

Chemistry

I hate chemistry,
It is mysterious and horrifying.
Some say that love involves "chemistry."
Love is chemistry.

People write of the beauty of love.
But what is beauty,
What is love?

Love is chemistry,
And in chemistry
You do not know whether
A reaction will softly bubble over,
Or explode.
Sending shards of glass flying.

The real difference between love and chemistry?
I can always study for chemistry.

Deathbed Fashion Show

Benjamin J. Cutler

When my great aunt was dying—deferring
dialysis for the comfort of a hospital bed

hospitably set in the living-room of her home,
toxins bypassing kidneys like bedtime shadows

leaking over horizon's edge to signal sleep—
her daughter-in-law sampled her wardrobe.

Stepping from the hallway door, having passed
from a closet choked by the must-of-memory

through the bygone bedroom, she stood on sorrow's
silence as a leaf-bare tree pregnant with the chatter

of hacking grackles: *So, how's it look?*
In her mother-in-law's muumuu, a cream silk

worn to corn-silk and a patina of cherry blossoms
aged to dusty potpourri, she smoothed hands

over full stomach and thighs and smiled with
teak-grained teeth. I got that in '66 in Hawaii,

my aunt said, It was so beautiful then. It's real,
you know. Take it if you want, whatever you want.

And she did. She also stayed after I left, I later learned;
she was living there for the week-of-dying to clean

Aunt's bedding and folds and weak waist and thighs
of bowels' release, a purge as dark and rich

as meconium—spoil of a body trying to remember
itself. With the strength and heat of a midwife's hands,

she scrubbed Aunt's skin white again. And again.
Avoiding nothing at all.

Moon Clippings for Birds

Moon looks like a thumbnail, she
                says from her seat,
and because she has never
                heard it before,

        the image becomes new in her lips.

        *

The night before, I had cleaned
                and trimmed her nails,
hands soft and still small enough
                to fit in mine,

        and piled each sliver into a nest.

She'd wanted to snip the last herself
                (eyes close to task).
When she'd finished, I pinched the
                nest to her palm—

        I'll take it out to the birds, she'd said.

        *

Tomorrow night that moon will
                be gone, I say,
Well, not really gone—but dark.
                Silence and then:
                It grows back. It always grows back, Dad.

On Teaching (Not Preaching) Poetry

Poetry went from fun to feeling like church.—11th-grade
English student

Don't feed your students stanzas
like a hellfire minister—mouthful
of verses bitter with consequence.

Rather, as generous host, invite
your guests to rest, lounged and languid,
lights lowered to a warm glow

so pupils widen as when a lover is in
sight. When they have forgotten home
and how to sit stiff as in a pew,

serve fresh water in clean glasses
so that they may see the clarity
of their gripping palms refracted.

Let them feel the coolness
on hands and tongues and taste
the sweetness of the spring

from which it was drawn.
Then, while lips are wet
and glasses still full, teach them

the miracle of tasting strong wine.

Grendel's Mom

"But now his mother / had sallied forth on a savage journey / grief-racked and ravenous, desperate for revenge."—*Beowulf* lines 1276-78, Seamus Heaney Translation

She wasn't a wrecker-of-benches
like her son—
or she had been
and put it away,
retired and tired,
to rest beneath
the giants sword.

Maybe she just wanted her boy
to come home,
away from the halls
and mead and meat
of men.

He's grown; he can take care of himself,
she must have said a few times,
her husky voice returning
from cool cavern walls dank with damp—
the echo a comforting confirmation.

When she lost
her Grendel to the Geat's pride,
an arm rent and kept for a prize,
when he returned, weeping for her,
a child again,
keening in a dying moment—

Modor, Modor—
she rose:
a mother in mourning,
a monster enraged.

Sometimes a son needs both.

Dead Bird Poem

Et le ciel regardait la carcasse superbe
Comme une fleur s' épanouir.—Charles Baudelaire, "Une Charogne"

One wing stretched to the sky
in a cartoonish bend as though to say
Why me? or What a world—
feathers fanned like petals.

This was at the place
where the two-lane meets the four-lane,
and as I waited to enter the highway,
I thought that I might write

a poem about this dead bird,
but then thought better of it,
how this kind of thing had already been done—
too often, perhaps—and why add to that

cadaverous canon. But were I to write
such a poem, I should make note
of those petal-like feathers
and maybe specify a flower

to sharpen the image: Echinacea,
but only the white variety trimmed with blue,
or maybe something with more
symbolic weight—like myrtles,

29

which I learned from Milton
represent death. Though, that would
perhaps be too pretentious—
more so even than an epigraph in French.

Were I to write this poem (and I'm not
saying I will), I would point out
how the breeze tickled the feathers into a quiver
so that a passerby might mistake this dead bird

for living, but that would be a lie;
no one would mistake its twisted form for life.
Poets lie too much, Nietzsche famously said—
so much, they sometimes believe themselves.

No—I am certain now that I will not write
a poem about this dead bird.
I don't even know what kind it is.
Tufted titmouse? House finch? Mockingbird?

Besides, I would need to find
the metaphor—something to give meaning
to the mundane in the tradition
of all great poetry, and this, I fear,

would not be great poetry
because I have no metaphor
for this dead bird, this flower
wilting on the concrete,

that was gone, leaving not even a stain,
when I returned at the end of the day.

Prey

Cathy Larson Sky

1   Finished with the gas pump, my husband goes inside to pay. We're in a rough neighborhood off 95N. Ragged men with brown bag bottles stand by the door. Truckers sit listening to short wave behind steering wheels, sunburnt left arms draped out the window.

I glimpse in the side view mirror my arm, shoulder, neck and chin, a quarter-torso. Heartbeat flutters beneath summer calico. Soft flesh quivers under fabric thin as tissue.

2   Rabbit suns, warming rosy inner ears. When clover blossom and birdsong fall away and shadows sigh *danger* she freezes bone-still, reading the air for wolf, coyote, fox. Or man. The glint of death.

3   One moonless night, I was cruising the Badlands with a lover who called me *doll baby* when a doe raced beside the open car window. Her head and neck were parallel to mine, her pulse a drum beat in the arc of tendon and rusty hide. Heat and scent of her wild body, terse rhythm of hooves, then she veered, swallowed by the dark beyond the head lamps.

Chickens

after Carl Larsson's *The Garden Gate* (1890-1899)

1   Inside the house there will always be a tin coffee pot, a dining room with gauze curtains, blue and white China, Delftware's echo. A vase of peonies. A woman with hair tied up Gibson-style, brunette strands escaping hairpins, shows off an apple-cheeked toddler.

Larsson's chickens cluck in the hay by the gate. Feed scatters, the hens rush. Hannah's alto murmurs an old Swedish hymn. She is my grandmother at eighty-five, in her night dress, feeding invisible childhood chickens. Eggshells, potato skins, oatmeal scrapings litter the grass.

2   Route 295 has eaten the front yard. Aunt Grace goes down the stone front steps in her bathrobe, wanders into traffic. She is tired of waiting *waiting* for the limo from the Swedish embassy. Queen Fredericka has flown to New York, anxious for Grace's counsel.

Outside the psychiatric wing, her three brothers huddle in a 1965 Plymouth Belvedere. Grace's doctor has asked them to come, wants to know could there be any truth to her recurring nightmare? The brothers agree, no need to reveal what they witnessed as kids, how their father tormented Grace as a child. *Besides*, they reason, *who would it help?*

3   Nestled at the edge of the broody patch, tail feathers gently curved, Larsson's rooster is almost invisible. Only his scarlet comb and mask betray him. The artist has chosen not to capture the rooster upright, his swinging wattle, his leathery feet and talons.

Fish Magic

~ Surviving the creative life

As you drop through the vault of silence,
you must learn the buoyant fall
of a bright Klee creature.

> Reflect the light
> of an invisible sun.

Ignore rumors that you are plankton.

> If you haven't fin or flipper,
> learn weightless ways
> of motion.

Hurried schools will switch direction
in concert, zig and zag:
Kandinsky angles.

> See, as they swim by,
> dark pin-points in each
> jellied gaze.

Should you be afraid, imagine a
corridor lined with Rothko,

> giant pelt of sea bears, prayer-
> soaked doorways to God.

Eye Light

~*from* "Child Ballad 10, The Twa Sisters," the English and Scottish Popular Ballads

1 *Weight*

They bring the drowned girl's body to Samuel, the miller's son,
and place it on a table. The girl's father pays
to have the body prepared for burial.
The mother hands Samuel folded linens.
Waiting by the door is the dead girl's sister.
Samuel sobs like a child when they are
gone. The dead girl is Eye Light, the village girl
everyone loved.

2 *Cloth*

Eye Light's long dark hair falls over the table's edge.
It's still damp from the pond.
Samuel gets a comb and brush from the stables. He works leaves
and twigs from the hair, then brushes it over and over.
He takes scissors and cuts it. He wraps the hair in a cloth.
While he washes the body, he grieves for William Tanner,
whom Eye Light promised to marry. He places a modesty cap
on her head, ties it below her chin.

3 *Ash*

Winter. By lamplight, Samuel loosens his fiddle bow
till the horse hair drops away.
He unwraps Eye Light's hair from the cloth, measures it
beside the horse hair. He cuts a piece the same.
He twists the ends to fit bow's tip and frog.
Samuel rosins the bow. White dust falls. Dark hair turns
ashy and coarse.

4 *Silence*

Eye Light's sister and William Tanner are married. Samuel comes
to fiddle at the wedding feast. When he draws his bow
there's a buzzing, like angry bees, below the strings.
The fiddle shudders,
moves like flesh.

Eye Light's voice shrieks through the hall
like a rush of bats streaming from a hollow tree.

It   was   my   sister. She pushed me   into the   water.

Sister rises and smashes Samuel's fiddle against the wall.

Salt

for the Newtown children and their staff

Because love is stronger than death
I light this candle for you.

Because stars do not know fear
cast yours away as you sail,
moonbeams, swift in the heavens.

Because this season you
too have been uprooted,
I trim this tree for you.
Pink, blue, red, yellow, green—
crayon box colors.

Because tears are salt
and blood is brine, the sea
shouts dark upon dark. The sky
blooms a silent, inky wound.
Armies of silver needles
drop, soundless, to the ocean floor.

Because these bones ache for you
and your pretty gifts that will not be opened

I open this place in my heart
where the briny tide ebbs and flows
and little starfish call your names.

Central Region: The Sandhills

Ruth Moose, Distinguished Poet

Mollie Porter, Middle School Student Poet

Esmeralda Garcia, High School Student Poet

Sophia Iannuzzi, University Student Poet

Douglas Chapman, Adult Student Poet

Leaving the Lake House with the Blue Door

Ruth Moose

Sunday morning
Early
From the back bedroom
Window I watch a silver mist
Rise and it's like prayers
Everywhere. It's a Blue Mosque
Of a morning and I write
In the stillness.
Where does my soul sit
In all this earth and sky?

With backpack and laptop
I walk west but say
to the tree beside the rocks
In the tall front grasses
We come.
We go.
We leave so little behind.
What gold of ourselves
If we are truly aware
Is what will live
In a word
A line
A time here
Remembered by someone
Who remembered.

Circe, On-Line Shopper

Circe in a Hostess Gown, Purple Satin Burnished gold
trim, tassel tie (Neiman Marcus $2329)

Circe knew the way to win them.
Wine in thick goblets, fruits in tiered epergnes,
pears and grapes, pomegranates, mangos and plums.
Cheeses, hard and soft, then champagne
toasts to their safe haven and brilliant leader
smiling on her right.

Before she led
them to the banquet table, they
drank in the joy of being celebrated,
the tapestries, the halls, the pleasures
awaiting. They marveled at the endless
tables laden shoulder to shoulder
with platters cradling tall beast. Oysters,
of course, bedded on ice with lemon lips
Tobasco hot enough to tingle their testicles.
Leeked soups and eggplant souffle, spinach
stuffed in tomato shells, garlic potatoes,
carrots in wine sauce and sweet
corn on the cob and off.

Everything appeared at the click
of her manicured nails.
Those sailors never knew it was their brothers smiling
red apples kneeling on platters, their skins

gleaming and crusty in the candle light, each morsel
tender and dear with juice.
Wine and more wine, stewards at every elbow.
then desserts: cheesecake, chocolates, peach pies, flan,
bananas flamed in brandy and cherries jubilee. Followed
by liquors. Those men swilled down the peppermint schnapps
like swines. They were fêted and fed, those feasting fools
while they slept their noses grew into snouts, their ears crawled
to the tops of their heads, peaked into points. They lost their
hair. Arms became legs and legs grew hooves, dark and split.
On the ends of their rumps, small tails twisted into curls.
When they screamed at the sight of each other, the sounds
were squeals of horror and alarm. Too late.
The fat from feasting lasts longer than a day.

Circe in a Cream Negligee with Matching Pom Pom
Sling Back Stiletto Slippers (Victoria's Secret $170)

Her gown was see through as dew,
shimmered like summer rain. She beckoned
them one by one to her black-laced lair
led them into a lower life: one they'd never
wished for, but learned to jostle their
way to get every morsel. She fed them
from her fingers, hibiscus, orchids, plumarias.
They licked her honeyed hands.

Circe in Jeans 7 for Mankind ($290)

They followed her over meadows
and through fields, stopping high on hills
to smell the sea which they remembered
only in their sleep. Teetering on their
trotters, they tramped after her. She
shepherded them past waterfalls,and muddy
ponds, ignored their grunting complaints to stop, stay.
At least in their pens, they lay on their backs,
four legs aloft. When they slept, they snored
like sailors.

And where was their leader? The only man
left among them? Escaped to the ship
docked in the harbor still as the winds
that lay dead in their wake.

Circe in a Royal Blue Suit (Armani $3950)

She was all business, bargaining
for herself, selling the kink-tailed porkers
to the highest raised hand, collecting
her sold and signing away their souls.
Then she bought drinks for the losing bidders,
sent them home with stories to tell.

All this while the leader of men slept in his sea tossed
ship.

Circe in Widow's Weeds (Neiman Marcus $2899)

After he left her bed, and she'd given him words
to win back his men into men, she wept for days
in the dark. Then she rose, dressed in long back,
hatted veil, matching gloves past her elbows, patent
pumps. She waved a black hankie, wished the strong
one a safe journey, wanted him back more than anything
in her life. But she waved hands that had fed and bedded
his creatures on her land.

She faced to flag the next load,
lure them ashore, show them what a good
hostess could serve and sell, how the magic
of her hands could work away any homesickness
poof, like a dream.

In the Bell Tower (Oxford England)

While the rest of the world
click fixed
before the flashing
neon of news
we wound the wedged steps up, up.
The stone beneath our feet, worn
in the middle. One at a time
we held the rail,
found those spaces
that spiraled
toward
the small,
old, cold
room at the top
of a world.

From the waist high windows
Oxford was a postcard of spires,
grids and trees. Turl, St. Aldates,
Jesus, New College, St. Mary's,
the cobblestones, all a burnished
dream.

There the tails of bells
dangled down.
The eight reached up,
grasp their task
in hand, pulled
to the numbered score.

And the bells rang out.
The giant flowers of sound
sang long past Evensong
into eight clock
and beyond.
The dusk fell fast,
wet as mourners,
at our feet.

The Wasps

Their bodies are burgundy brown,
shiny and intent. Bullet shaped.
With feelers they finger
where their nest has been.
That cone of pearls, empty now,
their young spun away. They circle,
disoriented. (I know how it feels.
Where is home? Where? Where?) One swipe
of the broom and I brought it down.
Great god that I am. Not. No mercy
in the laws of living. I am bigger.
I hold the broom. I own the porch.

They line up like soldiers
but there is nothing left
to guard, to fight for.

Coward that I am, I hide
behind the door, feel their wrath,
their buzz of anger, their question
why. I see their brown pain.
I can't claim
victory.

Daily Tasks of My Cat, Patrick

Early morning, it's hardly light,
he has bathed, breakfasted, eager
to be out the door, onto the job.
Petty businessman, hired gun,
serial killer, invisible briefcase
fast to his side, he straightens
his flocked tie, squares his shoulders,
and brushes past me, patient provider,
not even time for a quick flick of his tail.
Out to the commuter group at the corner,
he's one of the bunch, blends with the pack.

An hour later, (maybe it seems a day
in cat time), he's back for dinner, fast shower,
quick drink and a slow nap. He settles in
to snooze past the six o'clock news, wakes,
checks his watch, where has the time gone?

Evening, he's off to belly up to the nearest
bar with friends, smooze, cruise
the scene, stalk the moon, hide
under brush, climb neighboring fences,
jump roof to roof, scale walls,
sit on cars, screech to call owls.
Later he drags his fuzzy
carcass back to the hearth
and throws himself
at my feet, all merciful
and spent.

Trees I Have Known

I have talked to trees
And they have answered

In their own way.

I have befriended flowers
And they thanked me

In their own way.

I have held vines
And they let me

In their own way.

I have tamed towering shrubs
But they did not stay tamed but grew

In their own way.

How to Breathe

Molly Porter

many say it's simple,
without an inkling
of understanding
for those who lose
their breath within
a moment's notice
to stress.
focus, and relax
your muscles.
don't stiffen,
perhaps imagine
you are a griffin.
any magical creature,
soaring through the sky.
without that damned
double feature,
it's you, alone.
let your shoulders rise,
with a breath in
through the nose,
be careful, and
attempt to erase
any of those woes.
hold it,
like a rose,
with a smell
so pleasant.
let your soul

be iridescent
with an exhale,
let the air
leave you,
and sit there.
this poem is
not loud,
but important,
so be proud.

Passive

passivity does not have
to coincide with weakness.
push me over, i may tumble,
but not fall.
i am still me, and this is
who i am.
if you cannot see the me
inside of me, then
perhaps you'll never see.
soft does not mean weak,
people like me see things
differently from those
who would never flee.
fear is always here, but
so is knowledge.
intellect and a heart
have lead me from
the start.

Apprehensive

your lips are like
cherries, your voice
drips with honey.
luring, like the
sweet juliet
in a windowsill
to my apprehensive
romeo.
i'd love to be
the lurer, but
alas, i'm fear
filled and
freakish, so
i stay in my
shell, while
you break whatever
thin film covered
your beauty.

Waffle House

Sophia Iannuzzi

we woke up early,
wolling in opposites, side by side,
like a rorschach test.
we meet in the middle
but only occasionally.
                                        "what can i get you, baby?"
breakfast is on his mind, but i regret
to tell him there isn't much
of a choice in the area.

there is a salt shaker on the table during our first date.
unremarkable at first sight,
but his ocd says otherwise when he points its dented
tin lid away from him shyly.

the atmosphere works against him,
but his love of breakfast foods is stronger than his qualms.
"egg and cheese melt, please."
his sanity is melting
his eyes track
the movement of goings on
behind the counter in the grill area,   making   jokes
 an assembly line of greasy   poking   holes
foods.   in   yolks.

the most important meal of the day
the most stressful.
food sates his stomach   purell sates his mind.

There is No Softness in Florida

he changes the florida sun, with its warmth that makes
me feel like sepia postcards of oranges and taxidermy
crocodiles from a lost era, and which does not reflect
the holiday season despite the christmas lights on palm
tree crowns. i remember pouting at these crowns, at the
ocean, at the sand. they never reflected my fatigue.
there is no softness in florida, only sharp angles and
bright colors to which i felt foreign. these days the sun
does not cast such long shadows, it is high, as we are.
overcast kisses keep it from hurting my eyes so i may
see clearly. see, there are swamps in my mind i do not
visit anymore, like the everglades they are rife with
snakes and gators. thick and overgrown with lush
worry and the muck of insecurity. knowing they are
there is enough for me. i have spent too long in these
marshes that i have no desire to step into the mud and
wet my feet in silent sorrows. i will not eat the fruits of
the melancholy trees. in the florida of my mind he rips
up the splintered floorboards of the childhood home
lonesome made and replaces them in cherry wood, rich
and warm and smooth, easier for me to walk on when i
return to visit. much softer.

Best Served Warm

you are hollow
let me fill you
you are hollow
sugar,   darling?
let me fill you
you are hollow.
i fill you.
fill me.
teacups,
pouring
sweet teas with cream
milky warm kindness
soothing stomachs
back and forth.
back and
forth and
back.
neither empty,
neither full.
me, covering the cracks
in your porcelain
with my hands,
and you, mine
so we do not spill
do not waste
let me fill you.
fill me.
fill you.

Thirst

in spots where static once sounded
steadfast, i feel dreams
brewing. crazy notions
of lives we could live
if by chance you feel
similarly

laughter, a
drop of condensation
slowly slipping down a
glass of lavender lemonade
in sticky summer,
a fingertip at my spine,
pulling the thread of our fate
from the spool
longer and longer
and longer

smile.
bubbly cola
with extra cherry syrup
from the fountain,
sweet as sweet can be
popping when it meets
my lips
like static cling.
we cling.
no more static.
in sleep
despite your grumblings—

warmth, ecstasy,
soothes like richest
chamomiles
and me! a cookie
moving closer
soaking up the tea
of your person
leaching your warmth
a thief in the night.
imagine this, forever
if by chance you feel
similarly

i will read the leaves
of crumpled bedsheets
when we wake
and break away.
hoping for fortune,
and refreshment.

The Chime

Esmeralda Garcia

The day sailed on in a slow manner
The tick-tocks of the clock took their time,
moving slower than a sloth
The students sat still, like the chalk on the stand
They waited for the bell to chime. DING
Leaping from their seats the students headed home
The day zoomed fast, just to repeat the process again.

Ready For

Zion National Park, Utah

The drive was packed with excitement
My family passed the mountain and hills
We've seen a million times
Passed the cut open mountain full
of trailers and tractors
Leaving the mountains and trees
for the desert of cacti
Dressed in our best shoes, and clothes
Ready for the heat, and the crimson rocks
Ready for the uphill climb, and the whooshing water
Ready for Angels Landing,
and the sight of the mountains
Carved by time driving up the curved road
To reach the entrance
Parking the car and jumping out
Ready for the memories
that would last my family many years.

The Moment of Bliss

The Moment of Bliss is beautiful.
The Moment began the moment you confessed
Feeling of Bliss blossomed when you said it was true
The Moment continued when you said
You wanted me to be yours
Feeling of Bliss was real when you chose me instead of *her*
The Moment was when you said
it was okay if we had to wait,
You had understood Feeling of Bliss when
You said you liked my friends
The Moment etched to my brain when
You said you wanted to hug me and you did
Feeling of Bliss felt real when
You said you would sit with me instead
The Moment connected to my heart when
We met at the movies and you looked so happy to see me.
The Moment of Bliss is fleeting.
Feeling of Bliss wasn't so strong when you snapped at me
The Moment forever remembered
When you let *her* touch you and flirt
Feeling of Bliss fading as you became distant
The Moment hurt when
You blamed your parents for not wanting to be together.
The Moment of Bliss is beautiful but fleeting.

Disagreeing Views

Society defines what's normal and what's not,
But nobody ever thinks there is a bigger plot.
Disagreeing now is asking for disaster,
Want to change your mind? Better be faster.
If you don't agree you're a monster,
What was once traditional
is thrown out the window.
Freedom of belief and speech
means listening to what they say,
Everyone is human and respecting them
is important, especially today.
Those who dealt with the words of hate
from those who were prejudiced
Are now the ones giving the words of hate
to those who respect them but disagree.
Disagreeing views keeps
the endless cycle of split societies.
Agreeing views is not always the best end.
Whether you disagree or agree,
Respecting is what is more important.

Dad's Last List

Douglas Chapman

My father made lists—
  about everything—
  all the time.
Long after he died, we found lists,
  unfinished business,
step-by-step instructions,
small reminders of his
attempts to control a seemingly chaotic life.
But it wasn't so much the chaos as it was his feeling of being
  out-of-control.
With its inward growth of beauty
  and outward display of decay,
aging confuses the mind.
Lists were his way to tighten the sagging lifeline.

In the end, it was his failure to understand lists that led to a
  terminal diagnosis—
    the bank statement confounded him.
With his linear thinking scrambled
he was no longer able to comprehend
  life's direction.
Months later, as he struggled to hold on, as we
    tried in vain to convince him it was okay to let go,
I sat with him
  at the edge of his bed. I told him he had finished
the last item on his list.
He looked at me with wide,

innocent eyes and said,
"Really?"
"Yes," I lied, "you scratched it off this morning."

That satisfaction you feel when all the tasks on your list have been
completed had given him the permission he needed.
He died a few days later.
The greatest gift I gave my father was the freedom
to accept his last completed list,
the comfort of knowing that his next journey
would begin with a blank page.

Milkweed Journey

From a darkness beyond moonlight
a thousand downy milkweed seeds
spill into the summer night.

Freed of their podded home
they drift like layered lives
riding currents of primitive air.

I reach out to touch their faces
      —faces bathed in twice-borrowed light,
        faces holding ancient memories—
in search of some profound explanation.

Their pirated expressions echo only silence,
the silence of being.

On the Stillness of Trees

As I sit in silent meditation
    I am captivated by your peaceful presence.
Nothing exists for you
     save the stillness of being.
I call you many names,
   maple,
      oak,
         fir.
Your silent serenity,
    the strength of your bark,
    the porous canopy of leaf and limb
hold the truth.
While I am caught in my own thoughts,
you exist in no thought.
It is a lesson for those
    who are aware.
It is the blessed stillness of trees.

The Gift of Loss

Impressions
of myself
reflected,
mirrored images
of my ego.
Death
paints
the mirror
raven black,
traps each self-inspection
in the shallow,
narrow light
of fear.
Loss
peels back
the mirror surface,
permits
my soul
to see clearly
through
the window
I am.
Looking out,
no longer
myself,
only the pure
light of being.

Eastern Region: Hatteras

Amber Flora Thomas, Distinguished Poet

Tevin Aitken, College Student Poet

S.L. Cockerille, Adult Student Poet

John Gray, Adult Student Poet

Damaged Photos

Amber Flora Thomas

You get into puddles with the sky
and when this fails
pit your girl against an ocean.

Choices blur and make off with rooms
in the whiteness. Winged enough to manage
your red kimono's 37 cranes in various
trajectories while you make the coffee.

You as God with rattlesnakes
and His Admiral Death holding down the muscle,
headless and breath swollen.

You scattered in her facelessness
behind the screen door, not frowning, not joyous,
just working her hands in a dish towel,
folding them away.

You as ether, over-exposed bursting place,
dulling with these selves, spun by light
and dropped into shadow places,
forgotten as you put the photos down.

The Age of Forgetting

This happens with the rapture too.
Leaving your Birkenstocks and
brown sweater waiting at the chair
with a cold cup of coffee. A gift
of peacock feathers nodding in
a jar by the window. Served up

by science as brain atrophy. Shrapnel
misting cranial stars. Arias in oblivion
sending you into a remote outback
of lippy frostings and creams smeared
on spoons. Tripping until you tripped
into the white rabbit's belly fluff.

The rooms sucked away like cellophane
caramels and fizzy root beer pop. At first,
great-great grandmother Wickliffe and
our Cherokee in Tennessee appeared
as snapshots. Your newspaper route
in 1955. The stories you had to deny

undressed by cloud front. Your
disappearance like motion trapped
in a marble; the finite air bubbles
cruising that cosmos probably
breath. Little god raising your drunk,
smoked-out white flag at my entire life.

The Old Horse

He broke on linoleum flats
where he was made to play cowgirl.
Barrels and plastic cows he vaulted through
tumbled. His quarter split like a wing into the flank,
and his tail came away as well. Hollowness
all through the hoof.

The girl put her finger in the hole,
nicking her skin on a new edge, and thought
the horse trembled.

Leaning him against the barn, his three-legged
slouch facing a light pool in the hallway, she carried
his leg to her mother. "Fix this," she said.

Superglue later and his canter
tore through the blazing desert outside
the fence. Splinters showing,
the buff barrel racer stretched his neck
beneath her hand.

Always there then: her breath
trapped inside his body, that thin
pocket. The fragrant taste of plastics
and the mercury of loving him
so much, she could afford
to close away the song.

The Moon That Night

Having eaten your head clean off, my cat
drops your plump carcass on the doormat.
Between blood and purple clots, a bit of neck bone
insists on the air. I lean toward the sharpness,
get right up to the vacant white nipple, like milk
that has contested its cream and been deemed "fat-free."

Transparent like a baby's fingernail, the broken column
spills dead nerves. My cat licks her paw and smack!
your pudgy mass jumps, blood escaping into jute
threads.

White like the full moon that night I was twelve
and we snuck up the road. He opened his blue jeans
and thrust his blunt eye at me. It was this
or nothing, he said. I wish I'd chosen nothing.
Later, the moon split the road with redwoods
and I relented to my home. Exhausted,
I didn't swing my arms at the bat stealing moths
above my head.

I didn't wake again until you, little mouse
resting in the middle of "welcome," until my cat
in whose wide green eyes I see myself
leaning from the doorway, and I remember.

Pollen

—After D. H. Lawrence

As a person come through,
I say "I." In a halo of sun-stung colonizers,
minions with this one chance to claim a forest,
I lift my hand. Among soldiers,

my sweater is static and my upturned
palm a worship. Is this the door
and the knocking I must yield

myself to? Rain puddles collect
a glassy sage soup. I sneeze
and sneeze, but inside I know the offer is valid.

The neighbors call, "Friday, here boy.
Friday come." The cheer of dog tags
ignites from the bushes.

I need a great story today.
Tell me, do you still want ten children
and a musical number that will sell out the house?

I've scattered in every direction
so you cannot breathe me in.
I will not be breathed in by you.

A Wild Thing

If you thought there was sorrow in the bear,
its one-eyed gaze from inside her teeth,
shook against her jowls, and slobbered upon.

If you thought there was a better day
and more fun to be had, the bow
glued at its throat gone, the plaid
vest new with fringe.

Stolen from its shelf where dolls
and stuffed horses waited for parties
and a child's snug sleep to bloom
from its faux fur these clouds.

If you thought to pick polyester fiberfill
out of sunflowers, gather synthetic streamers
across the lawn and caught in the fence spikes
could wear you down.

Your house pulled open by this joy
and the brown dog dancing her flaccid kill
over the gate. So you tug the teddy bear
from her mouth and scold a story
that has put the sky on the earth again.

Here, saying, open that ragged gut of fluff
be gone in wild places, be grateful anyway
if this is the worst thing that happens
on your street today.

We Sit by the Bonfire

Tevin Aitken

We sit by the bonfire
And watch the salt water
With its many grains of sand.
The floating log is lost.
The rope from the boat screams let me free.
The sun says its goodbyes.
The waves hug the shore.
The trees with a cold towel
Cover the burning sand.
Footprints of memories,
The air filled with laughter.
The empty beer cans pile up,
Writing drunk, editing sober.
The black-necked stilts rest their tired wings.
The flock of ducks remains ugly
As their wobbling bodies march to slumber.
Heavy smoke from the bonfire
Chokes the fog, smells its crispy skin.
The crickets hide, singing a beautiful tune:
"You can't find me."
The stars are infinite.
The radio from the boat
Plays at a soft level.
The ocean tames my eyes,
Watching its many miles.
The switch in my brain went off,
Then I finally said it ... I am free.

Life is a Journey

Its ups and downs
Over hundreds and thousands of years
With nothing but suffering
People gone too soon,
Others got a chance but just wasted it
Some worship different gods
Their knees swelling from praying
I am plug to mic of the voiceless
The words to scriptures
The lost that found faith
The tears that hurt more than a bullet wound
The shells after a shooting
The one person that will admit
We are all racist, then people won't have a color
Keep your head high and let's all stand up together.
Let's remember we weren't born with hate in our heart.
We hate because
Love has lost its meaning
The soulless flesh, denied the feeling of being wanted.
Punishment is not enough.
No, you guys took the best thing in this world.
What is that you're wondering?
Love! Leaving Others Very Empty.
Shaming it so much that its only existence
Can be found in a very few,
And those few are scared to show it.
Leaving Others Very Empty....

You're the Judge

You're the judge
So judge me
Judge how I allow my daughters to get raped
The many white lies I heard
The many souls that I welcome home
Judge how I allow so many to be poor, while others rich
Judge the amount of suffering I put you through
Judge the abortions
Today you are the judge
So judge me
Judge the many corruptions I allow
Judge the countless murders
Can you hear the many tears?
You're the judge
So judge me
Judge me like how you judge my son
The hammer pounding the nail pushing
Judge the color of my skin
The length of my hair
Judge the walk in my steps
Just like how you judge each other
I mold such beautiful creatures,
But I cry lightning would strike twice
You weren't put here to judge,
But to simply love
Your mind full of such hatred

The First Knock at the Door was Strange

The first knock at the door was strange
Second was a damaged horse seeking
Freedom from its master
His shoulder was bleeding with the poison ivy
The bone in his left leg pointing
To the shooting stars.
His eyes with agony yet so gentle
This man stood at the door with warm water
Beating off the rooftop,
Dripping down his raggedy clothes

His structure not too far from mine,
A splash of water, brush of the teeth, spit of clean.
Whip of the face and a look in the mirror.
My mother's arms began to shake
As if she had seen God himself
The word "hurry" pinched my brain

Who is this? Tickle my toes
He fainted, my mother screamed
Compassion comfort her shaking hands
My knees kissed the floor,
His hands reached for my confused face
My ears opened up like a flower in spring
My heart kicking I could feel the cheetah running
The discomfort in his voice brought me goose bumps
My brain leaped into a pool of confusion

Why now?

The years they were the speck of dust forgotten
My struggles a dam as I squeeze
Through now I'm flowing water
So angry I bit my tongue
So lost I couldn't find my shadow
This man needled his way back to my tender skin
This man died in my mother's arms
This man was my father.

Moment of Happiness

I am not happy with my love life. The Grinch stole my happiness. No, I was the cause of that. Squeezing my fist so tight, but yet it slipped away. Like water pouring down the gutters. I couldn't stop it. My life layered right. The perfect sandwich. So I thought. I turned around and couldn't muster my way to stay faithful. Set ... Go! As my past chases me into the future, I dust myself off. Meet a new girl. From the first kiss she felt love in my lips. From the first stare, she saw loneliness in my eyes. From the first hug, my arms felt timid. As I embrace her, she tried to listen to my beating heart. It was quiet. How could I let her in? Knowing that sooner or later I am going to be the reason she leaves. So I close that door quickly, still hearing that soft knock from love. "Let me in." No, just leave me be. My soul is desperate for love, but still I couldn't figure out the formula. Then I had to start pretending and lying. Oh, the lies they had passion. I would grab love, dance with her, lay her back. Bring her closer. Whisper in her ears the lies, until they felt like the truth. Spin her around and continue dancing. That's how I treated love: keep on lying just because I was scared to love. Just living in a moment of happiness.

To the Bone

S.L. Cockerille

It was in '76 when he drove his motorcycle,
laden with weathered duffel bags, rolled-up blankets
and a handmade guitar case strapped to the sissy bar,

displaying behind him lacquered scenes
of curvy women, the Blue Ridge Mountains
and two little girls wearing fur coats on a sunny day.

The gilded wooden guitar case, with its necessary shape,
looked like a sort of joyful coffin riding on its head
for the sixteen hundred cold, wet miles

from Colorado to Virginia.
He wore thermal underwear and worn-out Levi's
and a surplus store fatigue coat over a jean jacket.

He was damp upon damp and had shivered for days
when he arrived early one morning,
resigned, relieved, tired.

The two little girls stretched open his clothes and blankets
on the morning grass, the red Virginia clay,
like offerings under the Virginia sun.

It was true, the sun had shone the morning he left Colorado,
as if to promise and plead, as if to tell a different story this time.
But he never trusted the sky over the Rockies—it was aloof

its mood seemed to belittle him, to taunt his quaint eastern ways,
his rumbling voice and slow accent,
his longing for a warmer place.

He'd grown tired of moody distance, of cold skies and chance
when he strapped every belonging he had to that motorcycle
and set out for home, for what he'd left behind,

for the mountains he loved, for the blood red soil, the little girls—
cold to the bone, determined
not to break another promise this time.

History's Glare

I have no intention
of telling my secrets.
If I did, where then,
would the world be without
those dark back stories
of my untoward feelings
and stealthy actions,
the words I've silenced,
the things I've put away?
For it ought to be apparent,
and I'm surprised it's not,
that the stories of nations
and the histories of rulers,
the longings of children
and wisdom of the ancients
hinge directly
on secrets like mine
remaining buried
in damp basements
and shallow graves.

Name

John Gray

I do like my name, John Robert Gray.
"Do you write Gray with an <u>EY</u> or an <u>AY</u>?" they ask.
"<u>AY</u>" is how I always reply.
How hard can it be to correctly spell a four-letter word? Wonder whether my middle granddaughter (whose first name is the same as my last) has similar questions about her NAME?
The most vivid memory of anyone addressing my full name negatively was my old college English professor (named Pikes Peak Paget) on that first day of college classes calling the roll and addressing me with the entire classroom listening, "Damn son, with a name like yours you'd might as well go home and pump gas!"
Wish I'd been more creative in answering his call and said "That's not how I wish to be addressed, I prefer that maybe you call me Bathroom Bobby of Color, or since I'm a numbers guy, maybe 464 (i.e. the number of letters in each one of my names)" would have been more creative responses. Instead, I simply replied, "Present, sir."
Guess I reacted as a shy 18 year old freshman might typically be expected, for at this point in my English college requirement, I just wanted to fade into the sad beige walls, get my C grade, and move onto what I perceived as more useful studies. But here I am today, so much different in old age, a beginning student of poetry.

Twenty Three

One of my bosses instructed that one has to give directions
at least 7 times for people to actually respond,
so here goes ... 23, 23, 23, 23, 23, 23, *and* 23.

If I were a famous sports person the 2 & the 3 would
be on my jersey.
Not because of all the pro athletes that wear those
digits,
Actually I don't care much for their arrogances.

My birthday is the 23rd
Married on the 23rd
Grandfather Billy died in 1923
and Dad died on the 23rd in '64

And Bill Shakespeare, like me,
was born on the 23rd of April ...
(he in 1564 & yours truly in 1946),
He died on *his* birthday—wonder what my
departure number will be?

And then again,
& most of important of all,
there's the 23rd Psalm!

DHS Class of '64

Graduated high school over 53 years ago—we've already lost nearly 20% of our 87 graduating seniors to a number of tragedies such as various cancers, accidents and even two suicides. Wish we were closer and cared about sharing our lives with one another. What year will the insurance company longevity tables predict that the '64 class is no more? My guess is that the sands of time for our entire bunch will run out around the 2045 timeframe (if indeed we're that lucky).

SERVING COUNTRY—DAY 1035—Tear Drops on a
Little Green Bird

Wee hours Easter Sunday morning—1973—Tripler
Army Hospital—

I received a phone order, "We need an inhalation
therapist in ICU, STAT!" Being the only technician
available, I answered the call, post haste. I was not a
trained respiratory professional (and only a lab tech)
but my duty was to respond.

ICU scene extremely sad—a beautiful 2-year-old
unconscious female on a Bird ventilator with
connections attached to her angelic baby face. 2 young
parents, 1 doctor captain, and 1 lieutenant nurse
joined me at her bedside. "We have no brain waves,
the Bird is merely allowing her chest to rise and fall,"
the doctor captain announced so matter-of-factly.

"What's the call, people?" the captain then questioned.
"Do we take her off this machine and let her go, *or* do
we keep this scene going on and on and on, like it has
been for the past 2 nights?" "Take those tubes and
mask off our daughter," replied the couple in almost a
unison brokenhearted voice. All eyes were on me to
perform the dreaded task.

And so that young life ended a matter of minutes after I flipped the Bird switch and pulled the electric plug. I removed the attachments from the child and pushed the little green Bird machine out of the ward. The lieutenant nurse and I spent a few moments consoling one another
by sharing sympathetic smiles and a brief touch of the back of our hands.

The nurse was not sobbing but I could tell she was hurting. Through her sadness, she said, "I watch people die here all the time but this one is the worst. It's just not fair that this 2 year old didn't have more of a life." As I was about to wheel my little green Bird out of the ward, a teardrop appeared on top of the machine. I never saw any of these people again.

And as I returned to the lab with my little green Bird, the single teardrop was joined by a mate. The sun was just rising on a majestic holiday morning. Instead of angrily questioning God, I humbly prayed that the 2-year-old soul was in a better place than this tropical paradise. I also prayed that we did the right thing by flipping that Bird, i.e. switch.

DS—THE END

End of the month our neighbor phones us
SHE's gone, DS is no more.
Halfway not believing the news
until we saw HER obit in the news.
Still hard to believe that DS is really gone

DS was the grand dame of Tarboro,
feeding and nurturing families
for many years by tempting us
with gossip, information, encouragement
and occasionally something even more.
DS was significant to diverse people and to me.

I did not always agree with HER spokespeople ...
Herman, Son,
Mabry, George, Terry, John, Calvin, Miranda
and an assortment more.
And I even made fun of HER sometimes,
Yet DS was a distinctive treasure for our little town.

SHE was and now is no more
Damn, I hate goodbyes—Damn Shame—DS
Why did you have to leave?
Believe we have nothing or no one that will ever
match YOU!

(Note: In case you don't know the identity of DS, it's a
description of *The Daily Southerner* newspaper of
Tarboro after her demise!)

Contributors: Biographical Sketches

Tevin Aitken is currently a senior at Barton College in North Carolina. He is a track and field athlete, born and raised on the beautiful island of Jamaica. "I am proud to be the person that I am today, because I am strong and focused on the life ahead of me. Making personal changes in my life is extremely difficult but with determination and reasons to want better, anything is possible."

Doug Chapman was born in 1951 in Chattanooga, Tennessee, but was reared in upstate New York. He graduated from Duke University with a Bachelor of Arts degree in history (1973) and from North Carolina State University with a Master of Sciences degree in horticulture. He opened Plantworks Nursery, Inc., in 1978, a wholesale nursery that specializes in herbaceous perennials, ferns, annuals, herbs, and ground cover. He also opened the Durham Garden Center in 2002. After many years as a successful businessman he sold both business in 2017. He is married with one son. And he remains passionate about gardening and nature, traveling, spirituality, and reading.

Originally from Charlottesville, Virginia, **S. L. Cockerille** has lived in North Carolina since the late 1980s. She received a BA in architecture from Virginia Tech. She writes both poetry and prose, and publishes her commentary on politics and society for her blog, *www.ShinyButter.com*. She was selected as a student poet for the 2016-17 North Carolina Poetry Society's Gilbert-Chappell Distinguished Poet series. One of her poems was recognized as a finalist in the 2017 North Carolina Poet Laureate contest, with North Carolina Poet Laureate Shelby Stephenson as the final judge, and two of her poems received honorable mentions in the Craven Arts Council 2016 Ekphrastic Poetry Competition, with poet Alan Shapiro as judge. Suzanna, who also goes by "Coco," is an active member of the New Bern's Nexus Poets, the North Carolina Poetry Society, the Pamlico Writers Group, and the Carteret Writers Group. She works as a blogger, freelance writer, and occasional website designer.

Mary Coggins is a senior at Mountain Heritage High School who plans to attend a university in North Carolina and major in English Literature. Mary began writing poetry when she was eleven years old after her dad passed away. She recently completed a year's service on the Board of Directors of SAYSO, a statewide advocacy association of youth aged 14 to 24 who are or have been in the out-of-home care system that is based in North Carolina. The acronym stands for Strong Able Youth Speaking Out, and the organization's mission is to work to improve the substitute care system by educating the community, speaking out about needed changes, and providing support to youth who are or have been in substitute care. Her interests include riding horses with her foster mom and reading and writing short stories and poetry. She also enjoys spending the day with her foster family, relaxing and playing old board games.

Benjamin Cutler was raised on a riverbank in the mountains of western North Carolina. He is a husband, father of four, and is a resident of Jackson County. Ben received his bachelor's degree in English Education from Western Carolina University and currently teaches English and creative writing courses at Swain County High School where he also serves as faculty-adviser for SCHS's Gay-Straight Alliance club. In conjunction with his work as an English teacher, Ben is an ambassador for the global educational non-profit *Narrative 4*, an organization founded by author Colum McCann that seeks to cultivate empathy through the exchanging of personal narratives. When he's not writing poetry or teaching, Ben spends his time playing with his four children, splashing around in the river, and trying to keep his honeybees alive.

Esmeralda Garcia is a Mexican American, originally from Utah now living in North Carolina. Having grown up loving reading and writing, it has shaped her point of view and the way she walks life. As an early college student, she is studying for an Associate degree that will later develop into a Bachelor of Arts degree in history. At her school, other students and she opened up a book club and became the main club founder. She has also been involved in the Beta Club by volunteering to help recycle after school. She has volunteered multiple times in local or school libraries and enjoyed helping out visitors of the libraries. Esmeralda hopes that when her education is over she can begin teaching because her future goal is to teach history. She wants to teach and make an impression on further generations to encourage them to make a bright future for themselves.

John Robert Gray Grew up in eastern North Carolina. He earned his BA degree in Managerial Economics and BS degree in Textile Technology from North Carolina State University. He worked as a Medical Lab Technician in the US Army (state-side) during the Vietnam War. He completed graduate work in textiles and participated in research at NC State following military service. His working life (post education & army service) included supervision and human resources management in manufacturing (textiles, power tool, & auto motive) industries as well as a soft drink sales supervision and special projects experience. He has been active in retirement with volunteer efforts for numerous organizations throughout the community of Tarboro, North Carolina. He is also in the process of attempting to write his memoirs to share with family members.

Sophia Iannuzzi is the daughter of a musician from Toronto and a schoolteacher from Long Island, New York. Sophia grew up in Southwest Florida, and later relocated to Bar Harbor, Maine. She received her BFA in English with a focus in Creative Writing from St. Andrews University in Laurinburg, NC. Sophia's poems and other works have appeared on the website *365Tomorrows*, and in volumes #11, #12 & #13

Gravity Hill. She was the editor of *Gravity Hill*, volume #13. She has one poetry chapbook out now, *Sophomore Slump*, a collaborative work with her sister. She is the recipient of the 2015 Nancy Bradberry Award for Poetic Form, the 2016 Editor's Choice Award from the St Andrews University Press for her story "Dead End," and earned an honorable mention from the 2016 NYC Midnight Screenwriting Competition. Her collection of poetry *Love Poems for the Socially Anxious & Other Maladies* was the 2017 winner of the Allan Bunn Chapbook Memorial Competition.

Distinguished Poet **Ruth Moose** loves to write. And read. And teach. Many of her students are publishing novels, collections of poetry as well as having secured teaching positions themselves. She is a prize-winning novelist, poet, short story writer, as well as a teacher. For forty years she's written poems, short stories, book reviews and columns and recently completed her second novel, the sequel to *Doing it at the Dixie Dew* which won the 2013 Malice Domestic Award and was published by St. Martin's Press in 2014. She will have a new collection of poetry *Barefoot in the Afterlife* and a collection of short stories *Going to Graceland*, both to be published in 2018. Originally from Albemarle, North Carolina, Moose graduated Pfeiffer University, then did her post graduate work at UNC-Greensboro. Before coming to teach creative writing at UNC-Chapel Hill, she was on the faculty at Pfeiffer. She now lives in Pittsboro, North Carolina, where she continues to write and teach since her retirement from UNC's Creative Writing Department. (From Ruth Moose website)

Pat Riviere-Seel is the North Carolina Poetry Society's Gilbert-Chappell Distinguished Poet for Western NC for 2016-2018. She is a poet, a runner, a woman who has lived long enough to have "past" and "former" prefixes for more jobs and volunteer positions than she can name without looking at a resume. She co-edited the anthology *Kakalak 2016* and is the author of two prize-winning poetry chapbooks: *No Turning Back Now* and *The Serial Killer's Daughter,* winner of the Roanoke-Chowan Award. Her most recent poetry collection, *Nothing Below but Air*, was a semifinalist for the Thomas Wolfe Memorial Literary Award. *The Serial Killer's Daughter* has been turned into a one-act play and performed by Shared Radiance Theatre. Pat has taught in UNC Asheville's Great Smokies Writing Program, and in 2012 she held a unique position as poet-in-residence at the NC Zoo. Before earning her MFA from Queens University of Charlotte, she worked as a newspaper journalist, publicist, and lobbyist. She lives in Asheville, NC.

Jade Shuler is a junior at Swain County High School who has been writing poetry since she was 13 years old and used poetry as a method of self-discovery and escape from problems she did not fully understand. In 2016 two of her poems were published in Speechless, an online publishing site associated with her school. She also read her poems at a Speechless gathering. This year she was selected to participate in a program with Narrative 4, an international non-profit organization focused on increasing empathy through the exchange of personal narratives. Jade enjoys reading, being outside, painting, and listening to music. She hopes to attend Lenoir-Rhyne University after graduation. "The idea that a big story can be told in the limited amount of space of a poem, is intriguing. It is also scary," Jade said. "I write poetry because I enjoy the language. I enjoy the easy flow that words can have when they are placed together."

Cathy Larson Sky's poems have appeared in *Western North Carolina Woman, Pinesong, Kakalak*, and the *Great Smokies Review*. Finishing Line Press published her chapbook, *Blue egg, my heart* in 2014. In 2015 she received three awards from the North Carolina Poetry Society, including first place in the Thomas H. McDill category. She has an MA in Folklore from UNC Chapel Hill. She is a traditional Irish fiddle teacher and performer, a former Our Lives columnist for the *Raleigh North Carolina News and Observer,* and the author of two unpublished novels.

Amber Flora Thomas is the author of two collections of poems: *Eye of Water*, selected by Harryette Mullen as the winner of the 2004 Cave Canem Poetry Prize, and *The Rabbits Could Sing*, selected by Peggy Shumaker for the Alaska Literary Series in 2011. A recipient of the Dylan Thomas American Poet Prize, Richard Peterson Prize, and Ann Stanford Prize, her poetry has appeared in *Callaloo, Orion Magazine, Alaska Quarterly Review, Saranac Review*, and *Crab Orchard Review*, as well as *Angles of Ascent: A Norton Anthology of Contemporary African American Poetry* and numerous other journals and anthologies. She is a

Cave Canem Fellow and faculty member. She is currently an Assistant Professor of Creative Writing at East Carolina University. Her third collection, *Red Channel in the Rupture* is forthcoming from Red Hen Press in 2018.

Acknowledgements

The following poems first appeared in the following periodicals/contests.

Cockerille, S.L. "History." 2016 Craven Arts Council's Ekphrastic Contest.

— —. "To the Bone." 2016 Craven Arts Council's Ekphrastic Contest.

Seel, Pat Reviere. "Desire." *Kakalak* (2015).

— —. "From the Almanac of Broken Things." First appeared on a poster as part of Poetry in Plain Sight sponsored by the Winston-Salem Writers.

— — . "The Bears." From *Nothing Below but Air*

— —. "What Emmett Saw." From *Nothing Below but Air*

Sky, Cathy Larson. "Salt." *Blue egg, my heart*. Finishing Line Press: Georgetown, KY (2014).

—. —. "Eyelight." *Kakalak* (2015).

—. —. "Fish Magic." *Pinesong*. North Carolina Poetry Society Journal of Awards (2015).

—. —. "Chickens." *Great Smokies Review*, Spring(2017).

A Note on the Gilbert-Chappell Distinguished Poets Series *

The Gilbert-Chappell Distinguished Poets Series originated when the Board of the North Carolina Poetry Society voted in 2003 to follow the advice of Fred Chappell, then North Carolina's Poet Laureate, who had written to advise the NCPS president about various approaches to take to further its mission to encourage the reading, writing, and enjoyment of poetry. The title is a combination of the two poets who supported this program: Marie Gilbert, a poet and former president of NCPS, and Fred Chappell. The program is sponsored by the NCPS and endowed by Dick Gilbert and Laurie Sanford.

Three Distinguished Poets, one each from the eastern, central, and western regions of North Carolina, mentor student poets from a middle school, a high school, a college/university, and an adult category not currently enrolled in a school program. (Home-schooled students are eligible to participate.) The Distinguished Poets work with their student poets over the fall and winter seasons that culminate in poetry readings in the spring. Each student poet will present one reading of his or her work in a local public library, sponsored by the North Carolina Center for the Book. Also, within these regions, each Distinguished Poet will present one reading with his or her students.

Each region has a chair and a committee to oversee the application process: Dr. Catherine Carter at Western Carolina University in Cullowhee, NC, represents the

Western Region; Dr. Ted Wojtasik at St. Andrews University in Laurinburg, NC, represents the Central Region; and Dr. Rebecca Godwin at Barton College in Wilson, NC, represents the Eastern Region. The Coordinating Committee of the GCDP that oversees all regions are Sally Buckner, Bill Griffin, Becky Godwin, Rhett Trull, Fred Chappell, and Bill Blackley. In the spring, Western Carolina University, St. Andrews University, and Barton College all host a major reading of their Distinguished Poets and student poets.

More information on this program can be found at

www.gilbertchappelldistinguishedpoetseries.com

* Information adapted from the North Carolina Poetry Society website

www.ingramcontent.com/pod-product-compliance
Lightning Source LLC
Chambersburg PA
CBHW070811050426
42452CB00011B/1992